GRANT WRITING

A Simple, Clear, and Concise Guide

CAROLINE SAVAGE

Copyright © 2017 by Caroline Savage

All rights reserved.

No part of this book may be reproduced in any form or by any electronic or mechanical means, including information storage and retrieval systems, without written permission from the author, except for the use of brief quotations in a book review.

Although the author has made every effort to ensure that the information in this book was correct at time of publication, the author does not assume and hereby disclaim any liability to any party for any loss, damage, or disruption caused by errors or omissions, whether such errors or omissions result from negligence, accident, or any other cause.

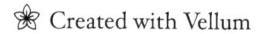

❦ Created with Vellum

For Steve, for believing in me...

CONTENTS

Chapter 1	1
Checklist 1	6
Chapter 2	7
Checklist 2	12
Chapter 3	14
Checklist 3	18
Chapter 4	19
Checklist 4	23
Chapter 5	24
Checklist 5	28
Chapter 6	29
Checklist 6	34
Chapter 7	35
Checklist 7	39
Chapter 8	40
Checklist 8	47
Chapter 9	48
Checklist 9	50
Chapter 10	51
Checklist 10	55
Chapter 11	56
Checklist 11	60
Chapter 12	61
Checklist 12	65
Chapter 13	66
Checklist 13	71
Chapter 14	72

Checklist 14	75
Chapter 15	76
Checklist 15	80
Chapter 16	81
Checklist 16	84
Chapter 17	85
Checklist 17	88
Chapter 18	90
Checklist 18	93
Chapter 19	94
Checklist 19	99
Chapter 20	100
Checklist 20	103
Chapter 21	104
Checklist 21	108
Chapter 22	109
About the Author	111
Also by Caroline Savage	113

CHAPTER ONE
Introduction

Thank you for purchasing Grant Writing - A Simple, Clear and Concise Guide. From the outset, this book is not intended as an in-depth discussion on the grant writing process. It is deliberately short in order to offer you support and guidance to get the job done. Think of it as having a skilled and qualified grant writer offering you a few words of wisdom to keep you on track. This book would sit somewhere between general grant guidelines and in-depth academic books. Both have value, especially the grant guidelines that are specific to your project - these are your primary source. You could call them the Funder's Law, if you breach the law you won't get the funding!

This book is aimed at those of you trying to make

sense of grant guidelines. In the following pages, you will find simple, clear, and concise advice to help you find your way around the application process.

The format of this book is set out in a similar manner to the information required in the grant application. This is a deliberate move to show you the grant writing process in action. Each chapter includes a question and a response and this is followed by a checklist which serves to highlight the key points in the chapter. The checklist can also be used as a quick reference by anyone else editing your work to make sure you have covered the salient aspects.

This book will give you the skills and confidence to search for funding opportunities, identify, plan, research, write and submit a grant application, and it provides information on the assessment process following the submission.

Note the change in language here: once an application is finished and submitted it is called a *submission*. This is an important term to remember, as the advice in this guide will relate either to action you should take regarding the *application* or action you might take as the result of a potential funder's decision regarding your *submission*.

As your skills improve, this book should still continue to be of value to you. You will be able to revisit key areas as you approach new, or more complex applications. It may also be used as a training aid memoir for you or for others you work with.

I wrote this book for one reason. I have been writing grants for over twenty years both internationally, and more recently in Australia. If you sliced me through the middle, inside you would find an ethics emblem relating to grants! I want applications to be carried out ethically and I am driven to support people in gaining the necessary information and skills to bring funding to those who most need it.

I don't see this process as a competition, although it does become competitive at the submission stage, but you know what I am saying. We are in this to help people.

In the many organisations I've worked with or for, the staff and volunteers in the business development/fundraising arena come from a wide and varied skill set. One thing guaranteed to normalise us all is applying for grants. The nuances of the grant-writing environment define a new way of thinking. The process takes skilled professionals out of their comfort zone and expects them to produce quality grant applications with little or no support. The time to identify, understand, and write, is quite often not factored into daily work schedules, and grants tend to be written at the last minute in almost abject panic. Let's face it, that panic normally sets in at the point you download the grant specifications. It doesn't have to.

I bring to these pages the experience of working in academic, not-for-profit, charity, and commercial (including social firms) organisations. In my experience, we were always time-poor, under pressure to maintain service provision, and often working alone, usually out of normal business hours, to get the grant submitted.

I believe that every challenge is there for a reason and from that comes the innovation for change.

Two years ago, I set an innovation in place and developed http://www.grantandtenderwriting.com for the local community where I now live. It is a place where I can reduce the burden of the grants application process on smaller organisations, who do amazing work with very little support, to give them a start in their research. Back then, I thought that the change was in getting the 'free grants' information in one place.

When the emails and Facebook messages came in, I soon realised it was just the beginning of the need that was out there. I received requests to train people, unpack opportunities, write grants and help develop strategic plans. There was no way I could meet that need on a one-on-one basis even if I gave up my day job and volunteered full time.

In short, I needed to unpack my head and share the process I used, to tackle the grant writing process in a way everyone could access, and at a price people could afford.

I've worked internationally and I've talked with colleagues all around the world. The grant-writing skill set is unique, but the geographical use of it is widely applicable.

Wherever you live in the world, I hope you enjoy this book. Once you've read it, please rate it, and if there's any further information you would like, feel free to email me via the contact link at my website

CHECKLIST 1

- Have you gained an understanding of the chapter layouts and checklists?
- Do you know where to go for further information?

CHAPTER TWO

The Grants Environment

Why should I care about the grants environment?

The funding environment is competitive; The funding purse is getting smaller and its drawstrings are tightening constantly.

If you examine the funding amounts available, and the requirements of the funding organisation, you will undoubtedly see that low-value grants tend to be open to groups with less formal structures. Sports equipment for sports groups, small pockets of funding for a community garden, and similar proposals. Once the cash needed is up over $5,000, the eligibility to apply requires more formality, such as information on organisational structure, or charitable status. Moving up to grants of $100,000 or more, you will see even more eligibility requirements relating to policies, procedures, quality, insurance and more.

By direct correlation, the applicant pool reduces as eligibility is tightened - and widens as eligibility eases.

I know from experience that a small grant of under $1000 that is open to community groups will be oversubscribed. I see this represented in *Grant and Tender Writing* Facebook statistics. Facebook reach of 10,000 views are not uncommon. The numbers reduce as the amounts increase and the numbers reduce further for niche areas such as academic funding.

Many organisations, especially those at grassroots level, are struggling to meet the growing needs of the communities and the people they help. Core funding from government is drying up, and more organisations and groups are relying on grant support.

Funding bodies have to be clear on their strategic aims, and they want maximum impact from their dollars. They reduce the eligibility pool of applicants further by adding layers of additional conditions such as tax concessions status or charity status.

There is a general funder expectation, especially at governmental level, for the 'not-for-profit organisation' to act as a 'for-profit in the not-for-profit world'. By this, it is meant that there is an expectation that the not-for-profit organisation will have robust business practices in place, will look to their sustainability, address the needs of target groups determined by the funder, and deliver clear and hard outcomes. In some cases, this is further complicated by the desire of the funder for applicants to deliver innovative projects and this can exclude 'non-innovative' projects that have had an enduring positive impact on the client base. In short, funders want to have a tangible return on their investment.

Funders now look at overhead costs and will not support organisations that are top-heavy. Consider a small charity, servicing perhaps 2000 clients, and a national charity servicing 200,000. The cost of a CEO may range from $150,000 at the smaller organisation to around $250,000 at the bigger organisation. From the point of view of the funder, the national charity would be seen to provide a better return on investment, as they should be able to show that more of the cash they acquire goes to service delivery as opposed to overhead costs. Value for money, need, and outcomes are key considerations for funders.

You may well ask 'but will the big not-for-profit deliver the better outcomes?' We are in a business world now. Harsh as it may seem, you need to understand what the funder wants, what they are prepared to pay for, what outcomes they expect for their money and how exposed you are if you don't meet the contract aims.

Funders are not being harsh but they are being realistic. They know that community need is vast. Conversely, there is only so much they can do, and their ability to assist is finite. For that reason, they concentrate on the needs they understand to be the greatest and the needs that impact upon their area of concern.

It is not unusual for those awarded grants to have to provide clear outcomes and acquittals, determined by achieved targets. Some of the formerly awarded grants money has moved to tender applications for that exact reason. Philanthropic money has, in some cases, morphed into social bonds where you have to demonstrate up front what outcome you will deliver. Underperformance is commonly contractually addressed with terms clearly withholding funds, and furthermore, payments and projects can cease, sometimes immediately, due to underperformance.

As a writer, it is important to understand the grants environment in your locality, the funders' expectations and peculiarities, and to apply to those who best fit your organisation, passion and client base.

If you are unsure of the funder's stance, check the projects they have funded before, the organisations they support and then realistically gauge where your organisation/community aligns.

CHECKLIST 2

- Do you understand the grants environment in your organisational area of concern?
- Have you researched your competition?
- Is your organisation financially streamlined?
- Do you have some idea of the percentage of your funds that reach your target group?

NOTE

If you want to learn more about global social bonds, check out Social Finance UK's Global Impact

Investment Bond Database at http://www.socialfinance.org.uk/database/

CHAPTER THREE

The Writer's Needs

What do I deserve as a grant writer?

I have already introduced you to my personal passion for ethics in grant writing.

Ethics is a part of the grants' process which you cannot ignore. The cost of writing an application for funds is usually ineligible in the actual costing of the project. For this reason, unethical organisations will ask grant writers to write for a success fee or hide the costs within the grant.

As a grant writer, you deserve more than just a possible fee for your work. Many factors influence the success of the application, such as the project, the track record of the organisation, or the ability of the organisation, all of which are out of your control.

You can write the best application in the world, but if these factors are missing, the submission will fail. Organisations pay staff for working. They do not place an expectation on them to get paid on some success six months ahead. Why should they expect that of you?

The other request often heard is to hide your fee in the grant. If this is an allowable expense, then that would be fine, and the word would not be *hide* but *cost*. Most of the time, grant writing costs are what we would call an *ineligible spend*. To merge them into the fee is unethical. If an organisation cannot afford to pay you to develop the grant, then their option to keep the cost down is to utilise a volunteer within their organisation. The same goes for you. Don't offer to write for a commission in order to win the grant. If you lower your ethics, you impact on grant writers everywhere.

What skills do I need?

The skill of grant writing is a unique one. It takes time to build up the expertise and confidence needed to tackle the writing without fear. However, with a bucket-load of passion for helping those in your community, it is a skill you can learn.

Your passion is an absolute prerequisite for your involvement in grant writing, and it will overcome many of the deficits that may be found by the funding assessors. Technical writers have their place in setting out the fundamentals of an application or in responding to a returned submission. They can provide clear text and technical information, but without passion, their grant submissions are not as compelling as those of a passionate writer who lacks technical experience.

Your passion needs to be met by your organisation. There is nothing more demeaning for a writer than to apply for funds for a project that is not genuine or is due solely to an organisational need for money. In these cases, a level of desperation will show in the application, and it will impact on you both during the writing phase and while you await the result. A positive mind-set is as important as a healthy workplace.

What else do I need?

It is important to ensure that you have the right environment in which to write. Ergonomic considerations and health and safety are a must to keep yourself fit and comfortable during the writing process.

If you are approaching grant writing as a business, ensure that you have the correct insurances in place. It may seem that there is little onus on you as a writer, but ultimately, if an organisation loses out on their funding they may choose to blame you. They may not have a case, but it is good to know you have limited your liability. Also, if you're entering other work premises, you may be liable if you stumble on the way to the coffee machine and break something!

CHECKLIST 3

- Are you content that the application is ethical?
- Have you set the level of payment for your work?
- Do you have the passion for the project?
- Have you set up a healthy workspace?
- Have you limited your liability?

CHAPTER FOUR

Where to Find Grants

Where do I find grants?

All grants information is free. Except 'free' isn't the whole truth. The information is posted out in the virtual domain for free, but finding it takes time, research and staff hours. I used to spend about three hours a day on my website Grant and Tender Writing trawling through emails and I posted three Facebook updates per day. Equate that time to an hourly rate and finding grants is expensive when you go it alone.

Some companies, for a small subscription, maintain a database of grants information. Their costs would need to be factored into your strategic plan for grant acquisition and divided by staff time. It may be that accessing the database and paying a yearly subscription is worth the investment. That's an organisational decision.

This chapter is for the smaller organisations who do not have the money to subscribe or who want to keep current on the grants environment. For them, I aim to share the process I undertake to find suitable open grants, that is a grant that you can apply to now, and future opportunities.

There are a few simple ways to search. Linking in to a site like mine that provides the information for free is a good idea. Undertaking a basic Internet search will yield some results. Subscribing to funders' ongoing emails will keep you up-to-date with media releases detailing the opening and closing of funding rounds. It will also give you an idea of projects that have been funded previously and what the funder is keen to support. Still on the subject of the Internet, Google News has an excellent feed where you can select keywords and receive daily email news articles meeting your criteria.

Although the above suggestions are a little haphazard, they do provide a quick review of opportunities and they will give you a starting point to work from. Your searches will capture closed, old, and current open grants so you are really throwing a fishing rod into a sea of information.

A more practical option is to look at funding

bodies either in your locality, or based on your area of need, and sign up to their mailing lists. The funders' sites may not only target the group you work with but should also give links to current research which can be beneficial to the grant writing process. The funders may also provide you with training and assistance to help you with your applications to them. Some of these funders will also have external links to funding opportunities. Search out community development sites too. If they are paid to develop your serviceable area, they will often have lists of funders.

You can also search for grants provided by corporate organisations, philanthropic entities, and foundations. These funders tend to release details about the grants on their websites and, as they know they will be oversubscribed, they may advertise only on their site and not elsewhere. The reason these types of groups are more beneficial to you is that they tend to fund projects which are about real people and that seek to find real solutions. They are free of state and federal strategic objectives. They are not looking to reduce the impact on the public purse but to show their corporate responsibility or their members' desire to give back to the communities they live in.

You will find grants in the most obscure places when you're in the right mind-set. When eating out at a restaurant, shopping, or involved in your usual work day, you will notice corporate sponsorship in action. Even better, you have the opportunity to speak to the staff and understand what drives the organisation.

Finding grants becomes like viral marketing. Each search flows to another, each research term provides plenty of leads, and soon your dedication to finding grants will pay off.

CHECKLIST 4

- Have you identified a site that provides grants information free or by subscription?
- Is the information provided in your area of need?
- Have you linked to state and federal sources?
- Have you widened your search to business, philanthropic and foundations?
- Have you set up a Google news search?

CHAPTER FIVE

You've Found One, Now What?

OK, I have my grant opportunity, now what?

All that searching has paid off. You have the grant to meet your needs, it is open, and the amount will allow you to deliver the project you have in mind. Now what do you do?

It's time to boldly step forward. No, seriously, at this point, you can freeze with all of the work ahead of you.

At this stage, I set up a folder and subfolders. I give the main folder the name of the grant and I name the subfolders as: *Funder Documentation, Research, Internal Docs, Drafts, Correspondence, Budget, Partnerships, Ready for Submission* and *Submitted*. This folder and subfolders are also backed up to Cloud storage, such as Microsoft365 or iCloud, on a real-time basis. This ensures that the application files are safe and accessible from any computer.

I then download all of the documents from the funder's website into, you guessed it, the *Funder Documentation* folder. This download would include information about the grant, eligibility, the application form, and any additional information they have and I would include a pdf of the webpage itself. This documentation is not changed in any way.

Next, I place a copy of the application into the *drafts* folder and rename it something obvious like *Caroline draft <app xxx>*. I put another copy of the application into the *Ready for Submission* folder and name this *<Applicant Organisation Name><Name of grant opportunity and number>*. The reason for the two copies is that I work on the draft copy for responses to the questions. This allows me to add in lots of additional information that can be edited and cut back to fit the response. Once a section is pristine, it gets copied and pasted into the *Ready for Submission* one. If you are part of a project team, this keeps one document within your control - not a bad idea when multiple people have input into the writing. More on that later.

With your *Ready for Submission* application document you can now go ahead and answer the organisational questions surrounding the central project questions. This activity provides an opportunity to add in your organisational information and will give you some certainty in gauging your eligibility for the grant.

At this stage, it is time to assess the grant. This involves reading through all of the documents to understand the grant process and the project requirements, and it will help you to get a feel for the funder's aims and objectives. It is also a time to assess who your competition may be and whether they may make a better partner, the additional research required, the due dates and the budget and funding available. It also allows you to check that you meet funding requirements, that you target the correct locations, that you have used the right methods, and that you can meet the date of submission.

Although *Funding* belongs in the *Budget* chapter of this book, I think it is important to make a point about the pool of funding. The funder may have $500,000 for one or more applications. I cannot tell you how tempting it is to apply for the whole funding amount. You know what I am saying!

I am going to suggest here that you have a look at the funder's previous rounds and see how they split that cash up. Did they go for one organisation? If yes, go for the $500k in funding. Or did they go for multiples with an average of $25k? If multiple, how many people did that $25k help? Divide the funding by the number of people helped and write that dollar amount down somewhere. Now assess how many people you will help and multiply it by that dollar amount.

I realised that I might have just removed the dreams of $500k, but my job here is to be the voice of reality...

CHECKLIST 5

- Have you set up your folders?
- Are they backed up?
- Do you understand the funder's requirements?
- Have you read the documentation?
- How much are you applying for in a dollar value, and is it realistic?

CHAPTER SIX

Does my Entity Fit the Grant?

Am I setting my organisation up for a strategic/reputational risk?

Organisational fit is an area where a reality test is required when submitting a grant. A key question is whether or not your organisation can meet the expectations of the awarded funding contract. It is an assessment of your organisational fit with the grant aims and with the grant funding itself.

If you stretch your organisation to deliver activity that is above its capability, you will fail to deliver what you promise. Risk assessments need to review the planned activity to identify issues in advance and to see whether there is the capacity to mitigate them. This issue is a book in itself but the message to leave you with is: 'do not apply for something that sets you or your organisation up for failure'. If it can't be delivered by you in the required timeframe, at the required cost and with the stipulated outcomes, even with mitigation risks in place, forget about applying. It is not worth building a reputation for failure. Go smaller, and look for funding to develop your project in achievable stages.

Don't apply to a funder that is unsuitable, or a 'bad fit'. For example, a health organisation with a strategic aim to reduce tobacco use in their clientele, or an environmental group with a desire to save sealife on the reefs, will be cautious about accepting funding from corporate tobacco/corporate chemical companies respectively. On the other hand, potential funding organisations could equally have a research or humanitarian aim to mitigate their impact on the organisation's client group. These are basic, but important considerations.

Can you imagine the fallout and the impact on your organisation if it were seen to be in bed with a funding organisation perceived to be the cause of its ongoing campaign? Now I appreciate that is a strong sentence, but reputational risks are highlighted by the possibility of ending up in the news with a sensational heading in the local paper, or as we should say now, in social media. You don't want to put your organisation in that position. At the very least, you want your organisation to consider all of this before they choose to apply. I might add here that if your organisation does make the decision to go ahead, this is one of the emails to keep in that *Correspondence* folder!

We now know the reason why your organisation benefits from knowing what the basis of the application is from a strategic and reputational point of view.

Do I fit the funder's strategic aims?

The funder is looking to see your strategic fit with them, and you need to address that now.

In the eligibility documentation, the funding guidelines dictate the requirements which the applicant organisation will need to meet, or they state the determined activities/organisations which are specifically included or excluded. Examples include, but are not limited to, a maximum organisational income limit, entity type, activity, and/or demographic limitations.

Like the applicant organisation, the funder will have a strategic map of their desired support areas and their determinants of needs to make that happen. In other words, the funder states, or has an idea of what is required for the applicant organisation to fit the strategic aims of the funder and to meet the eligibility of the grant.

Organisational fit is determined by mandated requirements regarding corporate structure type and income levels.

At this stage, you should check the funder's program documentation to determine what entity structure they are targeting, such as community organisations, not-for- profit organisations and, more recently, for-profit organisations where social benefits are fundamental.

There may also be a maximum income amount stated by the funder. This tends to come from funders who are keen to support grassroots organisations, or to support those with less income from grant applications.

It may be that the applicant organisation will need to seek external advice regarding their ongoing structure. The funding environment is changing. Social ventures that improve income may bring in much needed funding. Social ventures may also expose the organisation if the ventures fail and need cutting away from the group without impacting on other business activity. Commercial activities to drive sustainability may also impact upon income assessments for future funding, and upon maximum income levels.

Funders can have clear stipulations on locations. Whilst a National applicant organisation may need to maintain their umbrella of support of smaller independent entities affiliated with them, it may preclude them from applying for funding. Some funders will only fund an applicant organisation if the head office is in their locality. By contrast, the funder may allow for multiple applications from one National applicant. Always check this with the funder or their funding requirements before you invest in writing the grant.

Clearly, the above situations require professional input and advice. This is something to consider now, and in the future, as you continue your grant-seeking journey. If you have a good overview of the funding requirements of the grants you wish to access, the time to make these changes will be driven by the grants environment. I raise this now as I see not-for-profit organisations moving to a fee for service. Their business income will remain as not-for-profit, leaving them little spare cash for developing projects to meet need. Whether or not income is assessed, they will look well off, when in all reality, they will be surviving and not thriving.

CHECKLIST 6

- Does the grant meet the organisational strategic aim?
- Does my organisation meet the funder's eligibility requirements?
- Is the organisational structure correct for this type of grant?
- Does the organisational structure need review for longevity of funding options?

CHAPTER SEVEN

Research: What Are They Looking For?

What research do I need to do?

Research is a major component of the writing phase. The intelligence gained will add a level of strength not only to the application but in arguing the case for the project.

Most selection criteria ask for the need for the project to be demonstrated. And this is much more than requesting surface statistics. But let's start there.

Initial external and internal reviews of the relevant statistics will give you a benchmark for demographics and need. Sites, such as those of your country's Bureau of Statistics, will have geographical and demographic data linked to the last census.

The next step is to drill down for more recent information. Labour market information, for example, is released monthly and only a few months in arrears. Consider that it might be skewed to governmental agendas. For example, in the eighties, many unemployed people were being moved onto another type of unemployment benefit after ten weeks. The fact was that the statistics were not representative of the real issue. It meant that the unemployment figures did not represent those persons disengaged from the employment market, early retirees or those on disability benefits. The terms used to represent the whole working age group that was not working was the 'unemployed' and the 'inactive'.

The way that you research your statistics is pivotal. Look into them, but remain vigilant to the flaws in the numbers they represent and the background agendas influencing them.

Governments change in rapid succession. The skill is to have a robust understanding of your target group in your project to identify inconsistencies.

Internal experts may assist, and if you are fortunate, your organisation will have an evaluation framework with current and contemporary measurement tools.

Again, your critical mind has to step above your corporate or community alliances and it must scrutinise your organisational approach. While your project delivery may be effective, your project delivery may be compared with other organisations.

Key documents and research will provide you with some certainty in your approach, or they will highlight the need for any improvement or innovation required in your project methodology. It may be that you lead in the research and can demonstrate your track record to remain at the cutting edge, or it may demonstrate your reliance on out- of-date thinking. Strive to be current; funders like cutting edge innovation.

Funders also like value for money. Do your research on the value-set you offer, based on the wider community, the social/returns on investment, the hard and soft outcomes, the value for money proposition and the ability for the project to continue after the funding ends. All of this will support your application and add to the research elements of the grant. It will also provide a methodical approach to your work and will translate into ethical practices and defensible arguments.

The best proof of your worth will always be from the mouths of the people you help. You may be able to provide powerful vignettes from those in need to the funder at a level that elicits an emotional buy-in to the project. It will show, rather than tell a story about the project's effectiveness. It will provide a narrative to the issue you are addressing. It will show that your actions are achievable and relevant.

Research, as previously mentioned, is a major component. It is also a major time waster if you go off on a tangent. Plan for what you want to find, allow time to critically analyse the findings, save the documents to your research file, and report it back in a simple, honest and real way.

CHECKLIST 7

- What do you need to prove your case for funding?
- What are the avenues you can explore for contemporary and well-evidenced research?
- Critically analyse the source and agendas.
- Analyse your time and don't go off on a tangent.
- Keep documents and links in your folder and don't forget to save the link for citing in the document.

CHAPTER EIGHT

Research: Your Audience

I know I need to write to an audience, but who are they?

I struggled with the placement of this chapter as it could easily sit in the writing part of the book. I settled with *Research* because an understanding of this section flows on to Project Management and Project Planning. Let me explain.

When writing your grant, consider your audience, they are important. It is an easy mistake to get wrapped up in the process and the passion of a concept. It is also easy to miss the point on what *you* want as opposed to what the funder wants.

All funders have an agenda and they need an important reason to part with their cash. Carrying out research to understand the reason and the driver of the funder's mind-set will give you an idea of who you are pitching to. And it is a pitch. It is why your organisation deserves the cash over and above what may be a significant pool of applicants.

Governments, for example, are tasked with providing a multitude of services and will look at supporting their strategic goals and current agendas. The audience you write to is pivotal to your sanity as a writer. We speak of an audience, but any writer knows this is incorrect. The audience must be considered as one person who embodies the attitudes, emotions and fears of the group you are writing for. Sadly, for many of us in this employ, our audience has been determined internally.

A typical organisation has a process for review and sign-off. You may have project managers, strategic managers and a CEO involved in that process. Each will have their writing peculiarities and perceived requirements for the writing process. They may be so self-interested or so organisationally focussed and stuck in the process of the project that they forget who it is that you are writing for – and that entity is the funder, your audience.

It is your job as the writer to work with the project group in determining your audience. It is not easy, but it will impede your progress if you fail in this task. An example is as follows: Your CEO who is strategic, is delegated with signing off on your grant application. You know they will proofread for every missing apostrophe and every mistake, we all miss those sometimes and we may make grammar faux pas. You have an office-based academic who has developed the best and most innovative program. To add some personal conflict, you have a group of individuals about to lose their service provision and the staff who work on the project, face imminent redundancy. Sound familiar?

So, who is your audience?

It is a scenario we all dread. We sit at our computer frozen, cautious in every key stroke trying to please them all. When we get a draft together and attach it to the email, we wait for the critical feedback to come in and add to our dread. Each person reads from their perspective and takes the flow bit by bit out of the passion you tried to pass onto your audience.

Yes, I said audience. Not them (your work colleagues).

Each member of the applicant organisation has a role, and they need to understand that. The internal reviewer's viewpoint is valid, but the reviewer is not the grant writer. What they need to understand is that the real audience is the funder. The funder is the organisation who wants to see a project that gives them what they want, something new and innovative. They also want someone who will sort out an issue that keeps them awake at night.

It is one person who embodies the funder. This person can be a person you know or a fictitious person. Whoever you chose, they personify the funder for you. All the internal players in your organisation are probably passionate about the features of what they work on. They need to have the benefits squeezed out of them. Here is an example:

Me: At Grants Information, we post current information on grants.

Funder: Great, what's in it for me?

Me: 5000 plus people accessing grants information daily.

Funder: Good for you. What's in it for me?

Me: Grants Information receives no funding. We provide free information to 5000 organisational staff which allows them to build capacity and fund their service to assist the communities they serve. Can you give us a $1million to upgrade to provide a portal and get the message out to a gazillion people?

OK, so the above is a tongue in cheek response. It

does show what the funder is seeking. For a $1million grant, the funder's brand/mission gets to a gazillion people. For a $1million grant, a gazillion grant writers don't miss out on funding, and the cascade effect flows on to a gazillion communities and ten gazillion people. The funder cares about the benefit offered. The features of how Grants Information would offer such benefits are then presented later in the funding application.

Let's look at the funders and what they might require. Commercial funders will want a more straightforward 'what's in it for me' approach. They will want their services to align with their corporate brand and they will at least want to show their community participation and stewardship.

Academic funders require a different approach. There is an expectation that you write to the standard required in an academic paper. They are usually funding research and expect a professional approach.

Individual philanthropists tend to have a personal agenda. It may be a cause close to their heart or a lifetime bequest based on a love in their life. The fund may be run by them or for them. Regardless, the passion behind their cause is evident.

Philanthropic organisations are a mix of the individual and the commercial, under separate foundations, with predetermined target groups and activities. They are often oversubscribed and may require the building up of a more personal, networked approach before a formal application is made.

Community groups like the Lions, Rotary and similar organisations are more grassroots in nature and more responsive. They know their community, they want to help them and they are hands on. These groups like to see their funding in action and will often support the projects by providing volunteers.

What is clear is the need to understand your audience. Look into what makes the audience tick. Look at the funder's corporate information. If possible, do some relationship networking with them, so that your application is not a surprise. When writing to funders make it clear that you understand their aims and objectives. Respect their needs and the work they do to support organisations. Know their brands and their genesis. Don't waste their time by applying for something that does not meet their eligibility criteria.

Targeting your audience is a difficult part of the writing process. From your internal project team, set the guidelines up front, seek support, not criticism, and find a way to utilise the internal skill sets to strengthen the development of the project as well as throughout the application process.

Always remember, if the internal and external audience shares the same passion, you are writing to the converted. With the right networking and work, you will be colleagues and the impetus to support and fund you will be higher.

CHECKLIST 8

- Do you understand the funder's needs, innovation expectations and worries?
- Have you briefed the internal project management and project development team on the benefits they can bring to the process?
- Have you got one person in your mind who embodies the funder?

CHAPTER NINE

Research: The Software Needs

What software do I need?

This chapter is not the part of the book where I tell you that the best computer is a brand I use, and you need this and my software recommendations because I have an affiliate link.

This chapter is to make sure that you have a look at the grant overview to see what is required to apply and submit your application early on in the application process.

Within the documentation, there is usually a link to the submission portal or a request for the application form to be emailed. Rarely, the funder may ask for mailed hard copies. If this is the case, have a plan for the printing and couriers.

Be aware at this stage of the minimum Microsoft

Office version expected. If you use a Mac computer, open the application form and check that it all works for you. I have a Mac computer, and I find that it can cause issues with offline pre-filled document submissions. Issues have always been surmountable, but I do test them out early on so that I can work with the funder's IT department to find the 'workaround'.

If the form doesn't spell check, make a separate Word document to work on and copy the response across on completion of the writing and editing. Back this document up to a Cloud source.

The most important message from this chapter is to plan for the fact that on the day of submission, the internet version will freeze, your IT department will decide to update the network, the power will go out, the work will not save, or it will lose the text or something similar.

This is not me being a pessimist. I am a realist, and every grant has some panic element in the days leading up to submission. With planning, it has less chance to cause stress to you if you have contingencies in place, and plan to submit a day or two earlier than the submission date.

If it does go wrong, call the funder and seek an alternative method of submission. The funder should always be supportive if you have done everything to help yourself before the issue occurs.

CHECKLIST 9

- Do you know the submission process?
- Have you got the right software?
- Are you working on a separate document backed up to a safe source?
- Have you planned to submit early to miss the busy time when the system has the potential to freeze?
- Have you got a plan B (contact name and number) if there is an issue with the main way to submit?

CHAPTER TEN

Planning: Project Timelines

Managing the writing of an application and submitting a grant is a project in itself. It requires managing your time and managing the process of tracking the grant from identification to submission.

For this process, I tend to work backwards. My primary date is the date of submission (including the time of day stipulated). The reason I set this as the primary date, is that it is fixed and everything must work towards it.

Whilst working backwards might seem a weird way of working, it gives you the certainty of assessing the time you have left. Many grant writers are working in service provision, or other jobs, and grant writing tends to take a backseat to those.

Compounding this is the fact that many of us leave the actual writing to the last minute. This impacts on the quality of the application and the ability to attract funding for your project.

Obviously, depending on the organisation you work within, the times will vary and the level of complexity in the project management process will increase or diminish. Smaller organisations or volunteer organisations may have less red tape and bureaucracy to wade through. However, the project management process, and a stepped approach to the submission writing will serve to keep you on track and on time.

Now whilst this is project management, the level to which you manage, and the software you use is a personal choice. I do not use complex project management software for this process and I still use Excel. Using some form of tracking whether or not it is at a level of accountability, allows you to see project status in real time.

As good as your project management tools are, they still require you to sit down and write. Management tools are for your use and that of others, and it helps to have a project team, including yourself, to whom you are accountable.

So, what might your application look like? And don't forget, this is in reverse order.

- Formal date submission due
- Planned date of submission
- Formal sign-off by authorised person
- Editing
- Space to step away from application
- Writing
- Project overview and plan written and endorsed
- Letters of support and referees identified and gained
- Research completed
- Additional documents identified, checked for validity, and saved
- Time slots booked for writing staff, editing team, formal sign-off
- First project management group meeting booked - set meetings factored into project management plan
- Project plan commenced
- Project team identified and team meetings booked
- Project management plan completed
- Ergonomics, health and safety, and insurance in place
- Grant identified

Now read it from this end and you will see it does make sense!

CHECKLIST 10

- Is there an organisational project management tool already in use that you can utilise?
- Have you factored in all steps in the project management process?
- Is there sufficient time to submit on time?
- Is there a project management team to keep you accountable?

CHAPTER ELEVEN
Planning: The Project Plan

Why do I need to plan?

Planning is at the heart of the grant writing process. If you can work together with your team to hammer out the project plan, it will make the writing easier.

The size of your team and the number of experts who will want to weave specific features into the project will make this process more, or less, useful. Let me explain.

For any grant I work on, I map the project out on the back of an A4 envelope to see how it will work. While this may seem a bit ridiculous, it was ingrained into me in my first job as a project developer. We were at the start of the recycling era and had a lot of old envelopes lying around. It became my preference to visualise the project in one mind-map, so I could respond to the requirements of the project. I could also find the envelope in the research mess I seemed to naturally surround myself with. The envelope, or whatever you choose to use, is a great place to stuff key project notes into.

From that one A4 page, or big envelope, I develop the executive summary and I map out a project plan.

The project plan is essential, especially when you have a bigger team. The time invested in development and approval of that document will make the writing easier.

The plan includes, at a minimum:

- The name of the project
- An executive summary - write this last
- Organisational capability in this area
- Strategic impact
- Partners/referees/letters of support/vignettes
- The start and end date
- Project staff contact details
- The aims and objectives of the project
- The need for the project, including competition in this area
- The research and the gaps in research

- Target groups including ages, gender, demographics, and the proposed number you will target
- Target group outcomes and benefits
- Activity and timeline of the project
- Milestones
- Measurement and evaluation
- The project management team
- The staffing, and a clear picture of their work hours, their reporting and their educational qualifications
- Additional resources required, including premises, information and communications technology
- Relevant policies and processes such as finance for acquittal, and Human Resources for recruitment and screening
- Advertising and marketing including co-branding, if required
- Internal literature to support this project such as annual reports, track- record
- Additional anticipated costs to meet funder requirements, such as insurance
- Relevant policies and procedures

With all of this information written out in your unique voice and approved, the writing will flow, and other project development activities, such as budgeting will be easier.

Any subsequent changes to the plan due to, for example, budget constraints, can be factored in and activity scaled up or down before you write. It is a *live* document, and everyone can focus on what they want in there, and when you get to the writing stage, you know exactly how the project looks.

CHECKLIST 11

- Do you have a one-page overview of the project?
- Have you developed and gained approval (with all interested parties) for the project plan?

CHAPTER TWELVE

Planning: The Project Review

The plan is complete. I want to get on with writing so why review now?

With the project plan complete you can now review the organisational capacity to deliver the project on time and on budget. Organisational capability is a key question in whether the organisation can meet the expectations of a contract, if successful, in an award of funding.

Many organisations have experienced existing in an environment where their core activity is funded/has been funded by one stream of funding. Based on this assumption, it follows that the new activity requires the freeing up of staff and organisational resources, such as volunteers, space and overheads to meet the new grant, or it shows a need to bring in new resources to support the project activity.

Freeing up resources may seem a given, especially in this harsh economic environment. However, there may be gaps in the organisation's budget where activity is underfunded, where cost-of-living increments have outstripped current funding, or where the current funding does not cover the actual reach of your organisational strategic aims.

Stressors from outside of the current activity must be recognised. What is the capacity of your organisation to meet this new activity? Are staff and volunteers capable of meeting this additional need while maintaining their emotional well-being and maintaining a level of service? If not, what needs to happen?

Underestimation of time and resources are not uncommon. All grants place determinants on you to meet the eligibility and requirements of the contract. The funder assumes the organisation has considered the requirements, costed them, planned for them, can deliver the new activity, and can follow through from contract and award to acquittal of the project in the longer term.

This does not mean to say there is not an opportunity for adding value to current activity. There are always efficiencies to identify, under-capacity to fill and improvements in service delivery to make.

Reality testing at an early stage ensures fit on both sides, as does strengthening your position to prove project fit.

It is important to gather the evidence of your organisation's track record in the grant area. How many similar projects have been delivered, on time and on budget as well as meeting and exceeding targets? Locate the information and ensure that it is visible on your website, in annual reports and other organisational literature, and add this to your project plan.

With a strong track record in the target area, it follows that your organisation would have future needs identified, gaps in activity/service noted and innovative ways produced to target those needs. It is this type of approach that the funder will seek, and the organisation will need to prove to strengthen their application.

Sometimes an organisation does not fit the requirements of the funder. It is not necessarily the end of the application. Partnership and consortium applications can combine expertise and make an application under another lead applicant. A partnership is key to community groups who do not hold the requisite status, for example, charitable status, to be able to deliver projects. In plain terms, another organisation applies and sub-contracts activity to your organisation. The partnership will require clear distinction between both parties as to rights and responsibilities under the grant and it also requires a formal contract/Memorandum of Understanding.

CHECKLIST 12

- Does the organisation have the capacity to meet the activity?
- Does the organisation have the evidence to prove a track record?
- Has the organisation identified need, gaps in activity/service and innovation?
- Is a partnership, consortium or other lead applicant required?

CHAPTER THIRTEEN
Planning: Budgets

What is expected in the budget process?

Budgets are an area where you are at risk. Many people new to applying for grants may tend towards providing a low budget. While it may be a strategic move to take a loss on a project for a longer-term goal, reality demands that your budget is planned and accurate. There are many different factors to consider, and an accountant would be the best source of advice for budget planning. You will need to provide the relevant financial data to the accountant.

Have you built in redundancy?

If your organisation is in the service environment and has been for some time, staff may have been there longer than the project's existence. As staff length of service increases, and as they age, they build up entitlements which will cost the employer, once the worker leaves.

Back in early 2000, a European fund I worked with had been supporting projects for some years. It looked like it would never end and staff had been with projects for some years. Newly assessing countries to the EU came with greater social and economic needs. It meant that the proverbial cash cow funding dried up. It was an outcome we had not factored into projects, and the reality of where the redundancy payments would come from had to be faced. At that time, redundancy was not an eligible cost, and there was a considerable shortfall. The result was that my organisation was exposed to the loss. However, the organisation was also big enough to mitigate the loss by moving staff to other positions and letting natural attrition take care of the balance of employees.

For a small grassroots organisation, mass redundancies can be catastrophic. Check with your funder and assess the wage cost to cover the additional payments.

Have you considered the costs to exit?

Many factors, including rental of property and assets will affect the longevity of project life. Like redundancy, they need to be factored into the price.

The strength of the application and the budget

can be used as an exit strategy into a different model/mode/way. Think about how the project could move to a fee-for-service model, launch a social enterprise or similar. Funding isn't guaranteed but a decent business ethic will last a long time. If you can demonstrate the way in which your project can endure, i.e., by moving to a for-profit model, it will make the funding investment appear worthier.

Are there ways to add value?

Like exiting to a for-profit model, added value elements will strengthen the value of your budget. Overhead costs which are spread over a wider funder base will reduce costs, bringing in elements of fee-for-services will reduce the burden and will extend the outcomes that the funder can expect. Some funders will require a match-funded cash or in-kind element. If it is in-kind don't forget the value of volunteer time. Their time has a monetary value. Donations, fundraisers and similar streams can also all add to the support and add value to the project.

Have you considered staff time and the reality of workloads?

Don't try to save on costs by putting additional workloads on staff. Be realistic about people's capabilities and their work/life balance. This goes for volunteers too. Volunteers may give their time, but they are just as vulnerable to burnout, perhaps more so, as a greater expectation is placed upon the volunteer to help where funds are limited.

Have you considered penalty rates, coverage for leave, training?

Staff time is not always 9-5. Weekend work, night-work, callouts and allowances are all eligible, if the service you are applying for is required to operate on a similar basis. There will also be unplanned events where a non-crisis support service staff member will get called out at night. Where the government department funder dictates you accompany a client to the hospital in an emergency, then they will expect a provision in the budget to cover it. Additional staff costs are known, consumer price index and pay increment increases can be estimated and additional staff coverage for holidays or for staff development training are fixed. These costs need to be considered and factored in.

Have you factored in the other costs?

Insurance costs, information communication technology, vehicles and a wealth of other expenses associated with staff, volunteers and clients must be costed out. Some items may not be eligible. For instance, one funder I worked with would not allow asset purchases over $500. At the time, the cost of a computer was $800, and we needed computers for the project. The purchase restriction did not extend to renting, so we planned to rent the computers for a year. We negotiated a deal to get them donated to the clients at the end for their ongoing use. Ethically, we did not benefit from the deal, the funder approved the approach and it added value to the project.

Have you considered engaging a financial expert to review the budget?

It might cost a few dollars more to have your budget reviewed. It will cost a whole heap less than the potential loss to the organisation. This one is a no-brainer. Sure, keep the workload of the expert down. Do all of the groundwork, but don't cut costs in protecting the business end.

Have your costs in delivering the project come within budget?

With all of the planning, there remains the fact that staying within budget will be an ongoing activity for the life of the project. Auditors may be required to check the eligible spending, and there will be acquittals at fixed points in the timeline. Like everything else, they will need to be budgeted and managed.

What do you need to do now?

With the final budget complete, go back and align it to the final project plan.

At this stage, the budget and plan are distributed to the project management team for final approval.

CHECKLIST 13

- Have you factored in all possible costs associated with the project?
- Have you sought professional advice on the budget?
- Has the final budget been aligned with the project plan?
- Has the budget been approved?

CHAPTER FOURTEEN
Writing: Style

How do I know what style guide to use in the grants application?

Choosing the correct style guide for a grant is quite easy, and I will share with you how I work it out.

If the funder has a reference to a particular style guide then use that. Many though, don't.

Look at the questions on the application. Are the questions being asked in the second person, i.e., 'What will *you* do?' or are they being asked in the third person, i.e., 'What will *the organisation* do?' Respect the formal style of the funder by responding as they have written. Now, having said that, I am going to contradict myself and say you want the funder, the reader, to buy into your project. So... write in the first person, the 'We'.

With regard to style, what about the format? Are the funder's questions unjustified with regard to the print margins on the page? Or justified, like this book? You can follow their style, or be brave and make your text stand out. I don't have the answer. I do what I must do to get as close to the reader as possible and sell the project. That's the style I use.

Where I come up against issues is with a fixed-minded organisation. People who don't write grants sometimes believe every corporate publication, including grants, must be written in a certain style. I agree to an extent.

As grant writers, we are creatives and storytellers. We are more aligned to the *Ted Talk* engagement style than the organisational annual report. Good luck with telling a fixed-minded manager that though.

Perhaps this may help in your conversation if you have a fixed-minded manager. I know assessors who will exclude an application as they are of the opinion that the organisation hired a professional writer. In their minds, those without professional writers deserve the funds more. I don't agree and, as you know now from this book, grant writers do a heck of a lot more than writing.

We need our submissions to be read for impact,

we need to meet grammar and punctuation requirements, but we also need space to be creative and to sell the project.

You will find that you have to work around mindsets and negotiate change. You will also have to critically review your skill sets to ensure that your writing style is up to contemporary standards.

CHECKLIST 14

- What are the style constraints you HAVE to adhere to?
- What style have you decided will best bring the reader in and sell your story?
- Do you need additional training in storytelling?

CHAPTER FIFTEEN

Writing: Answering the Question

How do I respond to the questions?

If you have taken the advice in this book and filled in the main document, you are facing a screen with the central project questions before you. You have researched the application, and developed a project plan and budget that are both approved by the project team. You are ready to answer the questions.

Look at the questions and then map in bullet point form what you feel the funder is looking for from elements of your project plan. Highlight any areas in the questions requiring clarification. Contact the funder for any clarification you need.

Review the bullet points to see that there is no

duplication in your planned answers, or gaps in your responses to what they are asking for. The gaps are indicative of missed nuances in the questions and therefore, gaps in your responses.

With the background information and project plan, you will have the features of your project and the reasoning behind it.

You will have vignettes to add and can set up where these need to go. A vignette is a powerful way to convey the project message. A real-life story of someone overcoming adversity in their life through your organisation says more than a multitude of words.

Get active in the words you use. What reads better to you?

This project plans to deliver...weak?

The project will deliver...strong?

Talk to the reader as if they have given you the money and this is what you are doing with it. Be confident in your approach. You have worked on the project and know it is achievable.

Paint a picture of the issue in the area you are targeting. Provide demographic data evidenced to the funder's accepted source and research documents. Link to current strategic documents and exemplify where your activity fits the aims and how it differs from current activity. If you can show that it is innovative and exciting, this will add to the strength of your application.

Provide a narrative around the project plan. Demonstrate the nature of the project, the duration of the project, what you will do, why you will do that and how you would deliver the activity. Discuss the skilled staff you have in your organisation, when outcomes will be seen and measured, and the impact they will have on the target group, along with the strategic impact on the funder's aims. Express the return on the funder's investment that your project will deliver. Quantify the saving you can make within the project and, as a result of the project. Exemplify your capabilities to deliver this project on time, on budget, and for the benefit of the client group.

The funder will ask a series of questions throughout the application to tease out from you the information they require to make a decision. Each question is an aspect of the overview above. If you understand your project and the need for it, you will be able to answer the questions within the document. Do not start answering the questions until you can logically explain your project plan. By logically explaining, I mean that you need to show that you understand the aims, the objectives, the process, and the outcomes both during the project and as a result of the project.

Finally, make it easy for the assessor to score. Answer the elements of the questions in the way that they are asked. Making the assessor's job easier makes for higher scores.

CHECKLIST 15

- Have you mapped the questions and added in the vignettes?
- Have you taken the features from the project plan and translated them into the benefits to the funder?
- Have you evidenced the need for your project?
- Have you clearly stated your aims, objectives, project deliverables, and outputs?
- Have you responded to the funded questions as per their requirements, and with the assessor in mind, for every question?

CHAPTER SIXTEEN

Letters of Support

Do I need a letter of support and, if so, from who and in what format?

The funder will stipulate the requirement for letters of support. Letters of support provide an excellent opportunity to strengthen your proposal and they have become more important in the grant's environment. A recent grantor stated in their feedback that they were so oversubscribed with well-written grants, that their selection came down to the local and relevant letters of support.

Gain letters of support from:

- Potential participants/recipients of your project/service which state the need from their perspective

- Partners in the project detailing where they fit into your project and what services/projects your application will link into
- Leaders and advocates in your area of expertise
- Evaluators and academics associated with the project
- Movers and shakers linked with the funder who have the potential to strengthen the evidential need for the project
- People from the local area or target group

Don't be afraid to say it how it is. If you haven't had the money to invest in a facility and it is old and run down, let someone from there state, in harsh and detailed terms, the impact this has on them. The voice of the potential participant/recipient is powerful and has a human element that grants can lack. The letter of support will be unique, and it needs to be.

When it comes to standing out in the application pool, letters of support enhance your project. They show the partnership, your position in the continuum of support, your innovative perspective and the need associated with the project.

However, letters are something that are often

forgotten and often left to the end of the writing process. Frantic phone calls on the day of submission are stressful on you as a writer and on those supporting you. Last minute writing leads to rushed templates and letters of support with little emotive or supportive language. Negate this with planned requests at the project development stage, and save them in the right format to the Ready for Submission folder.

CHECKLIST 16

- Are letters of support required?
- Have you targeted the supporters to add the most value to your grant application?
- Are the letters of support unique and emotive to the funder?
- Are the letters of support in the right format, i.e., on a letterhead, signed and dated and uploaded for virtual submission, if required?

CHAPTER SEVENTEEN
References

Who shall I choose for my referees?

The funder may require references. Their relationship to your organisation will be prescribed in the funding documentation, or it will afford you freedom in whom you list.

If the reference is determined by the funder, cite those people listed in the desired relationship. However, if you have a choice, make a wise one. The easy option is to choose someone who likes your organisation. Perhaps situated in an organisation like yours or a person you feel is suitable. Think again. Step back from your organisation. Consider the grant from the funder's perspective. Is there a reference option from:

- someone respected by the funder?
- an expert in your project's field? This may be an academic and advocate or alliance/peak body leader.
- an influencer in the funder's portfolio or strategic aims? This may be a member of parliament, a senior manager in a government department or a peak body leader who knows your organisation and has been part of your history and achievements.
- a former funding body who can evidence your track record in the acquittal of your projects?
- an auditor or financial expert who can demonstrate your organisation's viability over time?

With all your referees, ensure you have briefed them on the project, sought their permission to act as a referee, gained their direct contact information and their availability to the funder. Spend time reflecting on the relationship they have with your organisation to gauge their understanding of their part in acting as a referee. Respect their commitment to you and drive longevity into that relationship to maintain it beyond the submission and into the assessment phase.

It is also pivotal to continue this into the new project, if successful, in order to build the relationship for future grant applications.

CHECKLIST 17

- Are referees suitable to the funder?
- Do they have an established relationship with your organisation?
- Have you briefed the referee?
- Have you set a plan to maintain the relationship with your organisation?
- Have you listed their current and direct contact information?

NOTE

If you have additional referees at the end of this process that exceed the number required for the grant application, ask them for a letter of support instead.

CHAPTER EIGHTEEN
Other Documentation Required

What other documentation do I need to provide?

A thorough review of the grant application will determine the additional information required. Each application has a backup checklist on the form itself, or as part of the grant information guide. In some cases, the requests are within the application questions.

It is a personal choice, but as I find the requests for the documents, I locate them and save them to the *Ready for Submission* folder and keep them in there in until the submission date. The frequent requests for documentation usually include asking for the last two or three annual reports, letters of support, insurance documentation, and other essential documentation about your organisation such as charitable or tax status.

One thing to be clear on in this section is the need to share only requested information. Funders ask for what they need to see. They limit this based on their assessments and tend to minimise this until they get near to selection. Additional information is not only cumbersome; it is disrespectful to the assessors in that it creates unnecessary review time. I get that it is tempting to add in information to strengthen your cause. But if you haven't made your case in the application itself, no amount of additional evidence can do that for you.

When you are preparing the documents, check the validity of the dates and the format required. For instance, if the funder wants a copy of a bank statement, they do not ordinarily mean a printout of your account from your bank's online account. Another example is with insurance where they may ask for $20 million liability. If yours is only for $10 million and you submit it without checking, you may have made your application ineligible. The other consideration is your own organisation's branding. Check that you have the latest version of the document, and not a draft that makes your marketing team plan your demise!

There are always grey areas in this process. The

funders always provide a contact number of someone who can advise you with the application paperwork. I do recommend that you back up any agreed changes to the process with an email from the funder. Make a note of it with the application to ensure it is apparent the changes were approved pre-submission. Save the email to your *Correspondence* folder too. It will be easier for you to find it again.

Some examples of additional permitted documentation are appendices, policies, project outlines, or delivery/project management timelines. These are typically allowable when an application has limited space for the response, but the word count isn't limited. It is a pain though as it can stop the flow of your response.

The final consideration is in the attachment itself. Data heavy pictures of documents have a habit of putting an email grant submission on a path to the dreaded bounce back. Quite often, email servers have a maximum limit on the size of attachments. While a full-colour photograph may look fabulous, a lower size/scale of the document will convey the information in the same way.

Like any part of the grant writing process, allow time to prepare attachments. Know the maximum size allowed and minimise the stress levels.

CHECKLIST 18

- Have you read the grant information and clearly identified the documents you must supply?
- Have you sourced the documents?
- Are the documents current and valid?
- Are they at the best resolution and size?
- Have you saved them into a file ready for submission?
- Have you identified the documents that add no value to the submission and incorporated the information into the body of the application?
- Have you negotiated with the funder for additional information and gained proof of the decision?

CHAPTER NINETEEN
Editing/Proofing

What is the editing process?

I have a confession here. Like all writers, when I put words on paper I place a little bit of myself on the page. I lie, it's a lot. The application becomes personal. There, I have said it.

The one thing that will be like a red rag to a bull when you have worked for days or weeks is a critical know-it-all armed with a red pen and their opinion of how the application should look. I love getting constructive feedback. I am happy for editing to happen...with a green or blue pen.

Be aware of this possibility in your writing career. Grants are a different way of writing. We do abuse grammar. We might move from first to the third person. We tell stories, and we elicit emotions from the reader. We have learned over time how to craft the application and, I hate to admit it, but part of that is conveying a part of ourselves.

When funders first moved to online grant submission, or at least sending it in Word via the email, they left the word count off the grant submission agenda. We wrote applications on reams of paper. Then, the funders determined a page limit for the grant. Obviously, they were sick of the length of the applications they received.

As writers, we made the margins so fine the text just started on the page. We typed in font size 7. We embraced the '&' and found acronyms and joined words together wheneverwecould. In those days, we thought to get the point across took a lot of words. And big words at that.

Since the advent of Facebook and similar sites, we know from the experts that people's attention spans have decreased. Plain English campaigns have us writing to be understood. It means we should be to the point and convey a concise message. A bit like this book!

The truth is writing advice has always said we need to edit down as much as possible. *Ted Talks* exemplify this and have also taught us that brevity is the way to capture the audience. Less is more, and this is the case at the editing and proofing stage of the grant. As is the passion you convey. The reader requires the feel-good factor as they read your application. Before that stage, you have an opportunity to fine-tune your application.

The editing process needs multiple reads of the draft. It requires the people with coloured pens and anal attitudes to grammar and editing. I follow an editing process before I send an application out for external editing. If at all possible, I deliberately leave a day or so between finishing the draft and starting the editing process.

Editing requires, in my opinion, three separate edits by the writer. The first edit examines whether you have addressed the questions, the flow of the document and the passion conveyed. The second reviews the format, the grammar, typeset, and word count. The final proof ensures every box is completed and allows a last run through of the checklist embedded within the application to ensure all documentation is ready for submission.

Once you have done your edits, understand that you will have missed glaring mistakes and there will be sentences only you will hope to understand. When we work on a document, the words are seen so often that mistakes are hidden in plain sight. To mitigate this, the document needs to go out to the project team for final review.

For the first review, ask the project management team whether your work captures the emotions, needs and hopes of the target audience your project will service. Ask whether you have captured their story? Ask whether the application engages the reader?

For the second edit, consider the person who wields the red pen with authority to assist you with this edit. As you have the subject matter in the right order, it is a case of seeking someone with a critical eye to micro-review the application. Team members with administration skills will quickly note whether you have answered with the first, second or third person and which is most appropriate. They will note whether the question and application form has the text justified or not and whether it may be appropriate to format it in the same style. They will also ensure consistency with the layout spelling, grammar, and organisational style guides. The second edit is also an opportunity to provide the funder's 'style guide' to assist with their editing process.

The final edit is back to you as the writer and ensures the integrity of the application. Here you will check the editing changes, the footnotes and references to ensure they are current and cited, ensure each box has been filled in, even if a 'not applicable' is required, and lastly, you will review the applications checklist to ensure documents are ready for submission in the correct format and embedded into the document if required.

The editing process is key to the planning and project timelines. As you complete more applications, you will get a feel for how long this internal process takes. It is always important to book people's time to assist in this process and to set expectations of them.

CHECKLIST 19

- Have you given yourself enough time after writing to complete the editing process?
- Have you provided your editors with some information on their role in the editing process?
- Have you booked their time in advance to ensure they can dedicate their energy to editing?
- Have you sourced the most skilled editors for each of the editing stages?
- Have you reflected on the process and length of time to complete future applications?

CHAPTER TWENTY

Sign-Off and Submission

What do I do to sign-off and submit the grant?

You've edited your document, and it is time to do the sign-off and submit the application.

The signatory to the grant application is sometimes determined by the funder, based on their authority/seniority in the organisation, such as the CEO. The reason for this is that the CEO can enter into a subsequent contract and has the organisational authority to sign-off on acquittals.

If you are the designated authority, this process is much simpler. If not, you will have followed the project timeline and will have booked the signatory to ensure they have time to read and sign-off on the application. Once you get it back from them, allow time to scan the declaration page if they do not have an electronic signature. Either way, this is the final document and will need to be in the *Ready for Submission* folder.

The next stage in the process is to check that all additional documents are there. The most important thing to convey to you is to give yourself time for the submission. I can guarantee you on the day of submission, Murphy's Law will trigger. Whether the funder's Internet portal has a glitch, your organisation has a power outage or aliens land, it will happen on the day of submission. The way to combat Murphy's Law is to give yourself time. I appreciate this is tongue-in-cheek, but I know from experience that if I leave the submission to the last possible moment my world goes downhill very quickly. If possible, aim to submit the day before.

When everything is ready to go, submit your application. Most funders will have an automatic response to acknowledge receipt of the application. If they don't, ask for one. Save the proof of submission in the folder entitled *Submitted*. In the same folder save a copy of the application you submitted and back this up along your normal Cloud backup or similar application. I also convert the submitted documents and proof of submission into a PDF, with the 'restrict editing' box ticked, and circulate this to the project management team. By putting it into a

PDF, no one can make any edits or changes to the document.

Now if you're anything like me, this is the time to congratulate the team, thank them for their support and find some way to relax until the next application.

CHECKLIST 20

- Have you identified the appropriate signatory or signatories for the application?
- Have you attached the additional documents required?
- Have you allowed yourself time to submit - expecting some element of frustration?
- Have you acquired proof of receipt?
- Have you circulated the final submission in PDF format and thanked the project team?

CHAPTER TWENTY-ONE

How Are the Grants Assessed?

What happens after I submit my application?

Assessment is the point where your application becomes a submission. There is nothing left that you can do to change the result. It's much like the time when you submitted an essay and waited for your grade so you could move on; it's frustrating.

It's also a time where the work falls on the funder, and I think you will see from submission dates during the year that the closing date tends to fall after holidays. It is no wonder the funding bodies ensure that pressure is not on their staff over a break, but ready for them on their return. If you have a submission date and it is after a significant holiday, set yourself the task of submitting before that date. Nothing will be done over the holiday with the application, and you deserve a break too.

Once received by the funder, the first step in the assessment process is to review the eligibility of each application. The funder's staff will review documentation, word count, the status of the organisation and other prerequisites they have determined the applicants must meet.

With so many applications, this is the easiest point for a funder to refuse your application. Some funders are more lenient than others and will call you to chase up documentation, but it's rare.

The second stage of the assessment process is to review each question against the set criteria determined internally, or in the documentation. When I have assessed grants, our first meeting was to set a benchmark score. The first few applications are scored by all assessors. Our scores and reasons for them were discussed, and a consensus on the score was reached.

Once we had an agreement on the scores to award, each grant was reviewed by three people and our scores added and averaged out. Any concerns were noted, and value for money equations worked out. When it comes to the budget, the funder had a value for money calculation. Value for money is usually an unknown calculation but it is commonly based on a way to assess all grants equally. For example, the funder may look at the sum of the hours the project will deliver over the project's lifetime and divide the whole project cost by those hours, giving a fixed hourly rate. In the situation above, when all applications were scored, they were ranked from highest to lowest, and those failing to meet a certain threshold were rejected.

From there, grants were appraised and recommendations added for funding. Some projects that scored low were bumped up in the recommendations if their project was innovative or deemed worthier. The assessors handed over the grants in this case, to the Minister, to make the final decision.

Whether your application is successful or not, it is always worth getting some feedback on the writing and quality of the grant submission. If you are successful, that feedback could be an internal process to know key areas where you feel your writing was stronger or your arguments were well-evidenced. If you're unsuccessful, the funder is the one to give some feedback even if it may be the case that they just had too many quality applicants. If that is the case, ask the funder what made the funded ones stand out?

You may not be successful in your first submission but keep trying. The funder has a finite amount of money, and many people seeking those funds. Keep improving your skills as a writer, especially after you've had the feedback and don't be afraid to ask whether the funder would welcome another application from your organisation.

CHECKLIST 21

- If you are aware of the applications' assessment process in the application documentation, write to it.

CHAPTER TWENTY-TWO

Final Words

It has been quite a journey, and I have enjoyed getting the information out of my head and into yours.

I hope the book has been as beneficial to you as it has been to me in writing it. Thanks to you, I have also refined my process in applying for grants and, for those of you who know me personally, I finally have my intuitive way of working mapped out.

Like me, you will continue to develop your style as a grant writer. You will evolve from submission to submission, and the grants environment will continue to ask you to do this.

If you have further questions or just want to give some feedback on the book, check out my Grant and Tender Writing website and feel free to send a message via there. I do answer my messages personally and get involved in the forum posts and discussions.

One last reminder. Please rate this book and provide feedback. It helps readers discover the book and your ratings matter — especially ratings with lots of stars.

Have fun grant writing and let me know how you go.

Caroline

ABOUT THE AUTHOR

Caroline Savage lives in Brisbane, Australia with her husband and is still writing grants and tenders.

Caroline is never happier than when she is developing a project that offers people possibilities. One that empowers people or communities to move from their current reality to one where their lives are enriched.

In doing so, Caroline has worked in areas that have truly stretched her own reality and in worldwide locations. Outputs include university research and development, education, social justice, health projects to social firm development and business innovation and heaps in between.

Over her twenty plus years developing and delivering projects, Caroline has brought in millions of dollars in funding, assessed grants and tenders on panels, mentored people and have developed a web community called Grants Information.

Grant Writing – A Simple, Clear and Concise

Guide is a way to give back to the community and to share possibilities, inspiration and knowledge with all of you.

Caroline loves writing, assessing, mentoring, coaching and strategic planning. She is happiest when working with projects close to her personal values.

If you want to know more check out

grantandtenderwriting.com
contact@grantandtenderwriting.com

ALSO BY CAROLINE SAVAGE

Tender Writing: A Simple, Clear and Concise Guide
Coming soon. See more at
https://www.grantandtenderwriting.com/tender-writing